My Life in Cars

Linda Strever

Linda Strever

For Jordan —
In gratitude for your
beautiful spirit,
your generous
support and your
keen insight.

With love,
Linda
2018

A Publication of The Poetry Box®

Editing & Book Design by Shawn Aveningo Sanders
Cover Illustration & Design by Robert R. Sanders
Photo on p. 27 by Tobias Huske

ISBN: 978-1-948461-12-2
Printed in the United States of America.

Published by The Poetry Box®, 2018
Beaverton, Oregon
ThePoetryBox.com

In memory of my father
Walt Strever, 1917-1978

and for Dave

. . . the darkness sur-
rounds us, what

can we do against
it, or else, shall we &
why not, buy a goddamn big car,

drive . . . for
christ's sake, look
out where yr going.

~ Robert Creeley
  "I Know a Man"

Contents

The Gospel According to Dear Abby

The three older girls who lived up the street exchanged
smirks over my head and laughed when one of them
said she was having, *you know, that thing that comes
at the end of a sentence.* My mother didn't say anything
when she presented me with the brown grocery bag:

an elastic contraption and a booklet explaining
with pictures that every month my body would make
a bed for a baby. When no baby appeared, the bed would
come out, and I could catch it with nice, thick *sanitary*
napkins, the *y* at the end of the word slanting dramatically,

a matching pink box bearing the same cockeyed script.
I followed the instructions, stretched the curling elastic
over my pants, stuffed the wad between my legs, hooked
its tails into shiny metal slots like giant needle eyes. I didn't
connect this bewildering gift—or my mother's peculiar smile

as she handed it over—with the doctor visit when he'd poked
at my stomach, looked up at my mother and said I was ready
for the big event. I thought he meant Thanksgiving.
A couple years later my friend Eileen and I, sweating
in our nylon baby-doll pajamas, pulled down our panties

and practiced inserting tampons. As she tossed
the cardboard tube toward the wastebasket etched with
roses, Eileen said she thought sex would feel like that.
None of it prepared me for sitting in the back seat next to
Theodore, my fourteen-year-old boyfriend, my hair teased

[. . .]

and sprayed hard for my first formal dance, my crinoline
stiff, the taffeta and lace of my dress crushed beneath me.
My mother did talk a lot about Eddie, the boyfriend before
Dad, because Eddie gave her a garnet ring, a gold watch, had
his own car. I didn't know what she'd say about Theodore's

hand cupped over my breast, the muscles in my arms
and legs knotted in the spotlight from each passing car.
In the front seat was Chip, who already had his license and
both hands on the steering wheel, Mary plastered against him
as if they were one body with two heads. There was no one

to tell me what to do with Theodore's hand on my breast
like the clamp Dad used to glue two boards together.
Mary had a reputation, which Dear Abby said never
to have. Dear Abby was really clear about that: once you
got one, there was nothing you could do to get rid of it.

1964 Chevy Impala

There's nothing like first love, metallic midnight blue,
my father's car, the first he bought brand new, the one
I learned to drive in, him screaming, both hands braced
against the glove compartment, sweat beading his forehead.
Clutching and braking were two opposing forces as we
bucked uphill to the stop sign, stalled, rolled forever
back, smack into the car behind us, finally came to rest.

He'd ordered it to his specs: the most chrome he could afford,
stick shift on the column, baby blue interior, custom floor mats.
Six cylinders instead of eight for economy, small for that hulk
of car, so he got overdrive to save the engine at high speeds.
He believed in preventive maintenance, had a valve job done
at sixty thousand miles, *Just in case*. License secure in my purse,
I washed and buffed that car every Saturday to earn the right

to borrow it, skipped driver safety class to park with my boyfriend
by the river, where I pressed against him in my peach and yellow
flowered pants, thinking we'd discovered something no one else
knew, until a cop knocked on the steamy back window, waved
his flashlight over our heads and sent us home, our zippers still
all the way up. By the time my father sold the car to me, he'd
downsized into a sporty Camaro, gold with a black vinyl roof

and gray velour bucket seats. Before he let the Impala go,
he insisted on a new coat of paint, taught me how to wet-sand,
and I made every square inch mine, not once, but three times,
the sandpaper finer and finer. Before I started commuting
to college, he showed me how to change a flat, had me block

[. . .]

the wheels, pump the jack, wield the tire iron, twist the lug nuts myself. I washed and vacuumed it each weekend just to please him.

When I married the boyfriend of the flowered pants, we traded it in on a used Volkswagen van, faded red with hand-painted interior, puffy cartoon clouds across a pale blue sky. My conscientious objector husband favored foreign cars, while Dad believed only in Chevys, though he never mentioned my betrayal, just as he'd never said much about a two-hundred-mile forced march through snow or six months of hard labor, lice and rancid soup in Stalag 4-B.

1969 Volkswagen Bus

I puked through most of my wedding day, in spite of my father's
cure—*the hair of the dog that bit you*—but by some quirk of luck

my dry heaves ceased in time, and I wobbled into my homemade
dress, set the circle of daisies on my hungover head, then waited

while the best man tracked the no-show Justice of the Peace
to the golf course and delivered him. Two hours late my father

handed me off to the groom, and we said our vows, exchanged rings
we'd bought at K-Mart. Our group of thirteen, like *The Last Supper*,

gathered around a single table, where the smell of fish made me
gag as I pushed dinner around my plate, smiled toward flashbulbs.

At some motel I slept right through my wedding night, and then
we headed south in the dull-red, sky-ceilinged VW bus. Somewhere

after the twenty-mile Chesapeake Bay toll bridge, I realized I'd
left my purse behind at the diner on the other end—complete with

a bag of pot, my license, my birth control pills, my keys, our cash.
Across the long expanse, all the way back—no land in sight—

my husband drove in silence while I looked at churning water.
I went in alone to claim my purse, didn't meet the manager's eyes.

We weren't as lucky when we crossed the Georgia line, where
the road narrowed from four lanes to two, the speed limit dropped

[. . .]

by forty miles an hour, and a cop was waiting. He called me *honey*,
my husband *boy*, demanded cash if we didn't want to spend the night

in jail. *We don't like your kind here*, he added, while he flicked
my husband's ponytail with his leather glove. We finally made it

to Orlando, where my brother-in-law and his wife had failed to land
jobs at Disney World. He filled vending machines instead, while

his bored and pregnant wife stayed home sewing a dress by hand,
chasing frogs and lizards from the doorstep with a broom. We slept

on the tile floor, waited in thirsty lines at the Magic Kingdom,
burned at Daytona Beach, dodged jellyfish and tourists in flat surf.

Somewhere between Tallahassee and Mobile I took over driving,
while my husband lay in back, moaned from sun poisoning. Exiting

a parking lot, I nearly killed us, managed to jam the shift into reverse
and floor it, just as the trailer truck went screaming past. We slept

in rest areas, on the shoulder of the road, at a motel somewhere
outside Wichita. My husband waited to mention the cockroaches

until after we'd checked out. South Dakota gave us Wall Drug,
the Corn Palace, the Old West Wax Museum, Mt. Rushmore,

the Badlands, what was left of Rapid City after a flash flood. When
we finally reached Yellowstone, we choked on campfire smoke

and exhaust fumes, watched people throw pancakes at bears
to lure them into photos, watched Old Faithful with half the U.S.

population, Yellowstone Falls with the other half. Our summer's
grand adventure shrunk to three weeks—we were *that* homesick—

we headed home, used the van to move our stuff from my in-laws'
basement to an apartment: three rooms, white walls, beige carpet.

1968 Rambler American Sedan

My father-in-law helped me buy it, opened the hood, jiggled
wires, kicked the tires, lay on his back and shimmied underneath.
Not much rust, he said. He was a body-and-fender man, whose
resulting emphysema had shortened his career. Instead, he

sold for Fuller Brush, and I still have folding scissors I bought
to be supportive. I drove it after months of unemployment,
stuck without a car, seasons of wandering a three-room apartment
looking for dust I might have missed, wedding presents stacked

neatly in the cupboards. I drove it to the jobs that didn't last,
the first one being McDonald's, where on every single break
the skinny, red-haired born-again tried to save me. *What DO
you believe in then?* he finally asked, chin thrusting toward me

like a righteous sword. *Self-actualization*, I jabbed back,
enunciating semesters of psychology like a curse. He rose
from the plastic chair, left his half-finished fries, his face
flushed with hellfire as if I'd blasphemed the entire holy trinity.

After work each evening, I performed ablutions: scrubbed
grill-smell from my hair and skin, scraped grease off my shoes,
laundered the two-toned nylon uniform in the bathroom sink,
rubbed the phantom hairnet from my forehead. I drove it to

the flower shop, owned by the mother of an ex-boyfriend who'd
moved with his new wife next door to my in-laws and claimed
we had unfinished business. He drove deliveries, while I shivered
in the giant walk-in cooler, slicing stems with a blade so they'd

drink more water, keep another day, every blessed stalk of flower
and greenery, my bleeding fingers swathed in band-aids. Half
my pay went for gas. Slow days his mother ordered me to clean
her apartment upstairs, warned me not to break anything. I drove

it to the insurance company, where I proofread fancy ads
and reports to shareholders, where the size and style of one's desk
and chair were determined by job title, my desk drab metal
with fake-wood vinyl top, my chair squat, armless. I didn't rate

cubicle or carpet, just fluorescent air, linoleum tiles. The woman
at the matching desk in front of me made her mark by forging
the president's signature, perfectly, on stacks of memos, letters,
certificates. One morning on my way to work, a cop pulled me over

for speeding, something I didn't realize the Rambler could do.
Eventually I carpooled, joked with an assistant actuary who had
her Ph.D. that it was like delivering ourselves to prison, except
they let us out each day, after we'd done our time. So her boss

in his teak-paneled office could set premiums, she analyzed
statistics with pencil and calculator at a desk just like mine—
though her chair had arms. Never did much rambling in the car,
despite its name. It was pale blue with gray interior, like my days.

1976 AMC Gremlin

We bought two of them, same mustard yellow, same
sawed-off back, so they looked like half a car each,
parked them in matching driveways, one on either side
of the front yard like bookends. The reporter for our
local weekly described our life as *serene* when he wrote
a feature on my artist-art-teacher husband, described
how we harvested herbs from the wild, made our own

wine, made sourdough English muffins from our friend's
grandmother's starter. We poured homemade sassafras tea
into our hand-glazed mugs, among our walls galleried
with watercolors, etchings, woodcuts, inside our windows'
green tangle of houseplants. In summer we canoed the lake
outside our back door, swam from our dock to the island,
jumped feet-first off the rope swing that hung from a stout oak.

In winter we skated before the first snow, cross-country skied,
ice-fished, our driveways neatly shoveled, quaint curl of smoke
rising from our chimney. No one heard me argue my way
to modern dance class each week, where I could move without
having to think, or saw my husband burn my art supplies
in the woodstove because I'd signed up for lessons he wasn't
teaching. When we'd bought our house, we'd consulted

the *I Ching*, and the two trigrams were *Water Dangerous*
over *Water Dangerous*. Anyone who saw us raking leaves,
me in the front yard, him in the back, might have thought it
sweet when he joined me, when he said, *I wanted to work
right next to you*, the tines of his rake nestling mine. One

birthday he gave me a silver choker, a seagull captured
in flight. The night I told him I loved someone else, he said,

I thought with the necklace, I could win you back. The next
morning I drove my Gremlin to work, while he drove his
to an out-of-the-way spot and put a hose on the tailpipe.
The police officer who arrived at the end of the day said
my name with a question mark. I remember a sound like
metal rattling. A friend drove me to the hospital, identified
his body while I waited in a hard red plastic chair. When

a nurse handed me my husband's wallet, I was surprised
by its weight. My mother-in-law said, *You'll have to live
with this for the rest of your life,* her sisters on the couch
like a line of crows eyeing a morsel. *Well, I never wanted
you to marry him anyway,* my mother said, adding how
terrible life was since my father died. My brother drove me
to the funeral home, where, along with all the men

in my husband's family, I picked out a casket. Afterward
my mother-in-law and the aunts planned what he'd wear
in the grave, rejected the clothes I'd brought, insisted on
their family plot. On the way home I looked at my brother,
and words came out of my mouth: *I want to be alive.*
A few days later he retrieved my husband's Gremlin, sold it
for me. When I was a girl and too afraid to try, I watched

my brother at the amusement park zip around in a bumper car.
I flinched at each thump, each sizzle and spark from wires
over his head. In funhouse mirrors I saw myself grow, shrink.
A few months after my husband's funeral I drove my Gremlin
to the suicide survivors' support group, where everyone laughed
when a woman told the story of how UPS lost her husband's ashes,
found them, delivered them to the wrong house, lost them again.

1981 Chevy Chevette

I traded in my Gremlin at my brother's friend's garage,
picked out the nearly-new, pearly-blue Chevette. The car
was quick, hugged the curves, plush bucket seat caressing me.
My lover didn't like my purchase—freaked out, in fact—since
he believed strictly in Dodges, years of sitting Zen not doing

much for his attachments. My other lover liked it fine, the feel
of the wheel and stick shift in her hands when I let her drive.
The evening they ran off together I tried to summon wrathful
gods to smite their dark and fickle heads but instead found
myself telling the full-moon sky, *Thank you.* The next day I

bought the car a stereo, loaded it with jazz tapes, and drove.
A few lovers later, after the biker and the photographer,
my sculptor sweetheart asked me for a ride to New York City
to check out graduate schools, but I was the one who ended up
there, where I studied writing poetry, where Allen Ginsberg

told me I wrote better poems before I came. Allen seemed to have
a thing for the woman in our workshop who'd made her living
as a dominatrix. All afternoon they sparred with words & rhythms,
and none of the rest of us could tell who won. For summer break,
I packed the car with camping gear, homesteaded on a friend's

vacant land in Connecticut until I got abruptly uprooted
by a hurricane. Back in the city, I drove it to my part-time job
tutoring so-called at-risk students, who said it wasn't school
they were sick of, just fearing for their lives. After graduation
I cashed out what was left of my student loan and went to Norway,

stored the car at a friend's, told her I was going there to fall in love,
but as it turned out, only one person paid me any attention: the man
who yelled across an empty restaurant in my direction, in English,
Women are nothing but holes to fill up. I did find my grandmother,
though, retraced her phantom steps along the eight-mile path she'd

walked in wooden shoes to church for confirmation lessons, heard
from my cousins' lips the quick in-breaths she took each time
she spoke, saw the farm she was named for, the schoolhouse where,
for a week each season, the schoolmaster arrived like a turtle, books
on his back. At the end of my trip, on the bus to the airport, a man

asked me, *Unnskylde meg, er den plass ledig?* I thought about
public restrooms in Oslo, how when a stall is occupied, the little
red bar over the lock says *Opptatt,* and when it's empty, the little
green bar says *Ledig.* So I said, *Ja,* and he sat down next to me.
Our conversation melted into English, all the way to the airport,

through Customs, through cups of coffee, and onto the plane, where
we ended up with a row to ourselves. A month later when I flew
west to visit, he wooed me with the Pacific Ocean, with sea stacks
and gray whales, sea otters and old growth cedars. When he flew
east to visit, I asked him to marry me. We drove the Chevette

to tour our old hometowns—his, oddly enough, the place where
my closest friend was born—months later, drove it to make
arrangements for our wedding, for the inn where we'd spend
our wedding night, exactly a year from the day we met. I sold
the car to my nephew, who parked at a boat launch with friends

and a case of beer, and somehow they floated into the river
up to its hood. He managed to get it out, but it never ran the same.
My husband and I drove a Ryder truck west with everything

I owned. It was August, the air conditioning worked only going
downhill, and the truck had a governor that didn't let it exceed

fifty-five miles an hour, made it lose power uphill in high gear.
Approaching the Continental Divide, I had two choices. I could
floor it, hope to miss the big-horned steer loping across the interstate.
Or I could stop, back all the miles down to the beginning, start over
in a lower gear. My husband still likes to tell how I floored it.

1986 Dodge Colt

Its one claim to fame was the night we slid into the ditch. My
safety-conscious husband stayed with the car, while I glissaded
the half mile home to call AAA, returned to find him moaning
in the passenger seat from the fall he took setting out flares.

Neighbors on that stretch of road didn't answer their doors, so I
sprinted home again to call for an ambulance—the ice gods
keeping me upright—returned to emptiness: no warning lights
flashing, no car sticking sideways into the road. I ran harder—

maybe I was mistaken, maybe it was over the next rise—when
I saw a tow truck deep in the woods, garish yellow lights still
turning, headlights glaring against trees, then the car facing
backwards in the ditch, enveloped completely in darkness. I

heard a radio crackle with static, spotted two dim figures standing
in the road ahead, one unmistakable. Soon the hill above us lit up:
ambulance, police, fire truck, the entire volunteer fire company's
worth of pickups, and a snowplow. Hours later we took a cab home

from the ER, my husband strapped in a brace to pull his shoulders
back, force his broken collarbone into a straight line. I retrieved
the crumpled car, drove it down the freshly sanded hill, past
the odd snow angel left by its own tires when the six-ton truck hit,

kept going, through the ditch and into the woods, mowing brush
and trees in its path. It was the driver's first night on the job. He'd
carefully followed protocol, parked atop the steep hill above our car,
left the engine running, set the brake, skidded and slipped on foot

[. . .]

to my husband, who managed to open the window a crack, explain
the situation. He clutched his shoulder to lessen the pain while
they talked, until movement beyond the driver led him to ask,
Is there by any chance another driver in the truck? The startled

guy answered, *No*, turned, started running uphill, yelled, *My dog
is in there!* Apparently he'd seen a lot of movies, cowboys leaping
on runaway stagecoaches, Superman stopping out-of-control trains.
Meanwhile, the truck picked up speed, aimed right for the car.

1988 Toyota Tercel

Dark blue with black interior, it's the car I sweated in, no air
conditioning and a heater that wouldn't shut off. I drove it
to the community college, where my least favorite student was
the baseball player who cheated on his Ethics final, tried to
convince me to change his failing grade: *You don't understand,
lady. This is a baseball town.* Among my favorites—the diesel
mechanic who came smirking into grammar class, moved a desk
to the front of the room, wrote *GOT SKUNKED* in big letters

on the blackboard, then sat beneath the arrow he'd drawn pointing
toward his head. He'd doused himself with every remedy known
to man but still reeked of the spray he'd encountered hunting elk.
And the retired logger who recited Shakespeare, Blake, Keats,
Whitman and a dozen others he'd learned by heart when he'd
sneak from the logging camp to the woods each night, read poems
to cure his stutter. Meanwhile, my biologist husband had a job
studying spotted owls. He roomed in a timber town, where

a restaurant sign boasted: *We proudly serve spotted owl stew,*
where the weekly news ran an editorial in praise of a patron
at a local bar who threw a mouthy tourist down a flight of stairs.
The tourist was quoted as having said, *I don't get the big deal
about spotted owls.* My husband came home each weekend
and cried for every stand of ancient trees he'd seen transformed
to stumps. I drove out one Saturday and we hiked together—
an owl landed, wings quieter than breath. That night we parked

on a logging road, walked until we heard soft mewling, followed
by a deep growl just below us. *Is that you?* my wise-ass husband

[. . .]

joked, then hustled me back to the car. My other favorite student—
the logger who arrived each morning in dusty caulks and overalls,
already done with a full day's work—decided to do his research
paper on old growth forests. Day after day, he caught me after class:
*Did you know there's a fungus that lives on the roots of mature
Douglas firs and nowhere else?* By the end of the quarter he was

lecturing his friends about the need for conservation. *Be careful,
or you won't have any friends left,* I said. *Did you know spotted owls
won't fly across clear-cuts?* he answered. The Tercel took me to my
next job, teaching in an army town, where students came to class
in their fatigues, called me *ma'am*, turned their work in on time.
Back when my husband served in Vietnam, I was on the other side:
saw protestors dragged by their feet to police vans, heads pounded
bloody against concrete, witnessed a cop in riot gear break my

friend's nose with his fist. Four days before the Kent State massacre,
I took part in a demonstration—my brother, somewhere on the edge
in his National Guard uniform, carried a rifle. It was the same day
my future husband nearly missed turning twenty-one. His boat
was traveling up the Cua Viet River, loaded with two hundred tons
of ammunition, when the barrage began. They couldn't shoot back—
under orders sensitive to public opinion—unless they radioed
up the chain of command for permission. He did the only thing

he could do: smashed the radio. Hitch-hiking after the war, he
made the mistake of telling a driver he'd just come back from
Vietnam. The guy slammed on the brakes, told him to get out, left
him in the middle of nowhere. During Desert Storm, I did the only
thing I could do: signed up to study conflict resolution. Day after day,
students disappeared from my classes, the halls full of emptiness.
I listened when my husband told me what his coworker said, *You
seem pretty normal for a Vietnam vet,* heard him cry for surviving.

1996 Honda Civic

It's the car I liked best, the one I had the longest, the only one
I ever named, *Sassy*, for the way it handled. Deep forest green,
its moon roof let me survey the sky, nuances of shade and light.
It came with a dent and spots of white sprayed on the fender
when the artist I bought it from ran over a can of paint, so I
never had to please the gods of perfection. My mediation car:

stuffed with bagels and training manuals I hauled all over town
as a one-woman Chautauqua of peace. The job was my all-time
favorite, trainer for the local mediation center, where *Laughing*
was a major goal in the strategic plan. I took the Civic camping
with a mediator friend, and we spent hours putting up the tent,
negotiated every single pole and stake, joked about the boring

reality show *Survivor Mediators* would make: no humiliation,
no one voted off the island. The car traversed my middle age,
carried me through wholly new terrain, with loss unwritten
on its signposts. I traveled with my love, with women friends,
alone—into the Cascade Mountains, to the edge of the Hoh
Rainforest, along the banks of the Columbia River, to bluffs

overlooking the Pacific—yet most of the geography was internal.
I evolved a theory that we grow to fill the landscape where we
find ourselves, and I set out to prove it. Asked to say the most
important thing she'd learned, a mediation student who'd struggled
to be articulate through forty hours of training stunned the group
to silence: *I don't need to change the world. I need to listen to it.*

2006 Scion xA

I quit dyeing my hair, let it go gray, traded scratchy contacts
for bifocals, bought a car hyped as the perfect choice
for the urban youth market. It came with an interactive CD,

narrated by a cheerful, spike-haired guy a third my age,
his upbeat demonstrations backed by incessant drums
and electric guitar. I chose it for the big windows that are easy

to see out of, high seats that are easy to get out of, automatic
transmission that saves my aching knee from having to clutch
in stop-and-go traffic. I bought it on the last healthy birthday

my closest friend would have—before she was diagnosed
with Lou Gehrig's disease, before the paralysis was so
advanced she couldn't eat or speak, before the doctor

mistook me for her daughter, though we were only two years
apart. The list of my dead keeps growing. They ride beside me
in the ghost-white car, the one I'll drive toward my old age,

equipped with six airbags to cushion the blows. On the first
anniversary of my friend's death, a shadow passed low
overhead, shook the car in its wake—as if an immense bird

stirred the air before it vanished. Last week a great horned owl
rose suddenly from the road ahead, wings lifting past
the headlights, over the hood and roof, into the widening dark.

Acknowledgments

"2006 Scion xA" was published in *Floating Bridge Review*, Number Five, 2012.

"The Gospel According to Dear Abby" was anthologized in *Godiva Speaks*, Godiva Press, 2011.

* * *

Thanks to the members of *Fusion* and *Team Awesome* for their thoughtful feedback on these poems.

Praise for
My Life in Cars

"*My Life in Cars* by Linda Strever is at once a history and a poetic memoir, punctuated with poignant nostalgia, comedic vignettes and soul-searching heartbreak. Each vehicle transports the reader along back roads and highways of the struggles and triumphs throughout the poet's life; a road filled with unexpected twists and turns that eventually lead to wisdom and perspective. Entertaining and enlightening, Strever takes us for a trip of a lifetime. As she puts it, 'we grow to fill the landscape we find ourselves in.' Sit in the back and watch her eloquently full landscapes slide by. It's a deeply satisfying road trip."

~ Patrick Dixon, author of *Arc of Visibility*

"While Strever's collection offers vivid portraits of cars as its title suggests, at the heart of these poems are the experiences, by turns harrowing, tender, and mundane, that forge a rebellious young person into a contemplative adult. Her writing is crisp with physical detail, through which we catch glints of understated emotionality. 'Never did much rambling in the car/ despite its name. It was pale blue with gray interior, like my days.' Strever doesn't sentimentalize tragedy, but gives it to us kindly, like a good friend who knows that life will always alloy great pain with joy. 'The list of my dead keeps growing. They ride beside me/ in the ghost-white car, the one I'll drive toward my old age,/ equipped with six airbags to cushion the blows.' Reading these poems is a pleasure that will leave you feeling wiser for having been invited to share in hard-won lessons of a life not your own."

~ Emily Van Kley, author of *The Cold and the Rust*

[. . .]

"Each make and model in Linda Strever's *My Life in Cars* narrates an unanticipated stop on one woman's ultimate American road trip, spanning forty-plus years from coast to coast. Poignant and bold, these poems move me to reconsider how the cars we drive transport our stories, recasting our daily lived experiences into the dreams and tragedies that inhabit every Memory's Lane."

~ Sandra Yannone, author of *Maiden Voyage*

"Who would have thought a single symbol could generate an entire life out of ten poems? What motif for a maturing American woman could be more telling than the car, the 'auto'? Linda Strever reflects on focal points of her life, anchoring the emotional, the devastating, in the mechanical to make them not only real but possible to describe. Strever, as always, is mistress of poetic narrative. There is not one word too many, yet no ambiguity. In '1996 Honda Civic' she writes, 'I traveled with my love, with women friends, / alone—into the Cascade Mountains, to the edge of the Hoh/ Rainforest, along the banks of the Columbia River, to bluffs/ overlooking the Pacific—yet most of the geography was internal.' The collection moves from youth through loss to a level of acceptance with deep sensuality and sexuality. Not only do I know more about Linda after riding with her in Ramblers and Impalas, I understand more about my own road."

~ Joanne M. Clarkson, author of *The Fates*

About the Author

Linda Strever grew up in Connecticut and earned a Bachelor of Science degree in English Education at Central Connecticut State University. In her mid-thirties she moved to Brooklyn, New York, earning an MFA in Creative Writing at Brooklyn College, City University of New York, where she was awarded the Louis Goodman Creative Writing Scholarship.

Her poetry collection, *Against My Dreams*, was published in 2013. The collection was a finalist for both the Intro Series Poetry Prize and the Levis Poetry Prize from Four-Way Books, the New Issues Press Award in Poetry, and the Ohio State University Press Award in Poetry.

Her novel, *Don't Look Away*, published in 2015, was a finalist for the Eludia Award from Hidden River Arts.

Winner of the Lois Cranston Memorial Poetry Prize from *CALYX Journal*, her work has been a finalist for the Hill-Stead Museum's Sunken Garden Poetry Prize, the *Spoon River Poetry Review* Editors' Prize, the *Crab Creek Review* Poetry Award, the A. E. Coppard Prize for Fiction, as well as in the Provincetown OuterMost Poetry Contest, the William Van Wert Fiction Competition, and the Summer Literary Seminars Fiction Competition.

Her poetry, fiction and nonfiction have been published widely in journals and magazines, and she is a Pushcart Prize nominee.

She has worked as a proofreader, editor, graphic artist, teacher, trainer, and mediator and lives with her husband in the Pacific Northwest.

[www.LindaStrever.com • www.Facebook.com/LindaStrever]

About The Poetry Box

The Poetry Box® was founded in 2011 by Shawn Aveningo & Robert R. Sanders, who wholeheartedly believe that every day spent with the people you love, doing what you love, is a moment in life worth cherishing. Their boutique press celebrates the talents of their fellow artisans and writers through professional book design and publishing of individual collections, as well as their flagship literary journal, *The Poeming Pigeon*.

Feel free to visit the online bookstore (thePoetryBox.com), where you'll find more titles including:

Keeping It Weird: Poems & Stories of Portland, Oregon

The Way a Woman Knows by Carolyn Martin

Of Course, I'm a Feminist! edited by Ellen Goldberg

Giving Ground by Lynn M. Knapp

Broadfork Farm by Tricia Knoll

The Poeming Pigeon: A Literary Journal of Poetry

Psyche's Scroll by Karla Linn Merrifield

Womanhood & Other Scars by Rebecca Smolen

November Quilt by Penelope Scambly Schott

and more . . .

CPSIA information can be obtained
at www.ICGtesting.com
Printed in the USA
BVHW04s2204230918
527871BV00018B/50/P